C000103874

500 FANTASY WRITING PROMPTS

ERICA BLUMENTHAL

Copyright © 2020 by Erica Blumenthal
    All rights reserved.
    ISBN: 978-0-6488502-0-5 (Print)
No part of this book may be reproduced in any form or
by any electronic or mechanical means, including
information storage and retrieval systems, without
written permission from the author, except for the use of
brief quotations in a book review.

DEDICATION

To my readers - remember, it's never too late to start
writing. Just start, and don't look back.

CONTENTS

CHAPTER ONE

Introduction

I wrote this book for my readers who just love writing and writing prompts. I wanted to write a small book to supplement what's already available on Amazon and to help you focus in on fantasy writing specifically. This book is to help you if you're stuck, or to give you a prompt from which to start writing.

Writing prompts can be a great source of inspiration for when you're struggling for ideas. Even browsing prompts can spark your own ideas for a story, or you can use the prompts exactly as they're presented.

Anything goes. And you get to decide!

You might be wondering about me; I guess you could say I am still an aspiring writer. I've been writing since I was about eight years old. I love fantasy, sci-fi, and adventure stories. When I was small, I wanted to write children's books and I loved Choose Your Own Adventure books. I even wrote my own choose your own adventure about a UFO landing in my backyard. Unfortunately, I have since lost that first manuscript (in notebook form).

Right from a young age I read all the young adult and adult fantasy I could find. I loved Diana Wynne Jones, the Redwall series, Tolkien, Feist, and now especially Neil Gaiman. I loved the weird and strange stories like Tales from the Crypt, Roald Dahl's odd fantastical short stories, and the mix of thriller meets horror meets fantasy which is found in so many young adult books, such as Christopher Pike's, and the Point Horror/Thriller titles.

Above all, I just love a good fantasy story, in any form it comes in. Ideas come easy for me, I've realised. It's writing them that's hard. So here are some ideas for you, my reader, to help start, continue, or help finish your fantastical story.

Happy Writing!

CHAPTER TWO

How To Use This Book

Here are some tips to help you use the prompts to your advantage. Remember - there are no rules when it comes to working with writing prompts.

1. Use the prompts to ignite an idea within you. You don't have to take them as is, just take what you like out of them, take the idea, character, anything that you can use as inspiration, to spark off your writing session.
2. Ask yourself questions if you're having trouble getting started... "Who is this character? What do they want? What do they need? What or who is standing in their way? What will happen if they don't get what they want/need?"
3. Aim to write 100 or 200 words or if you'd rather set a timer for 10 or 15 minutes or even 5 minutes and write to that, come what may.
4. Check out Holly Lisle's post on **"writing to a writing prompt"**. Paraphrased, she says, you need to have a Character/Subject and a Conflict. From there, you can create any story you desire.

5. A way to use the prompts, if you are practicing regular writing, is to do one each day, for a set period, perhaps as a "writing exercise" to start of each writing session. Pick a section and start making your way down the list.

6. Try Freewriting. Flip through the book and choose a prompt at random and write it even you hate it. Your hesitation may prove to spark an excellent idea for a short story or something longer.

I have broken this book up into 5 sections; the first four on different fantasy sub-genres and the last section on fantasy title prompts, including; fairy tale and myth & legend fantasy, epic fantasy, modern fantasy (including sub-genres such as Paranormal and Urban Fantasy), and other more general fantasy prompts (including other fantasy sub-genres). Within each section there are two types of writing prompt:

1. The first is a typical writing prompt, with typically a character, setting and a conflict. You might even get a villain for your protagonist. Sometimes one or more of these elements are missing. It's then up to you to create the missing pieces for your story idea.

2. The second set of prompts are titled "story starters" and indicate a style of prompt that typically contains a single line of text or dialogue, designed to spark a story in your mind or on the page within a timed writing exercise. These typically don't have a character or setting, but usually the conflict or situation. Again, it's then up to you to build out your story idea.

Remember, for both style of prompt, take what you like, and disregard what you don't. You never have to use the prompts as is.

I have tried to group these 500 prompts under relevant sub-genre headings, but it proved a difficult exercise, so I tried my best. There are many that cross sub-genres, but I hope you can easily find the prompt you want. Don't forget to use the search tool (if you have the ebook) to search a certain keyword you might be looking for.

CHAPTER THREE

100 Myth & Legend/Fairy Tale Fantasy

Prompts

On the following pages are fantasy prompts falling
under the general heading of Myth and Legend and
Fairy Tale Fantasy Prompts. These are my favourite
types of stories. In this section I've included prompts
that involve our common mythical stories, legends,
and fairy tale themed story ideas. Here you will find
your gods, goddesses, kings, queens, and princesses,
and different takes and twists on classic fairy tales and
myths.

50 Myth & Legend/Fairy Tale Prompts

1. After 20 years of living with your curse, the witch who placed it returns. "Aren't you curious how to remove it?" she asks, puzzled. You shrug. "I'm used to it."
2. There's a war brewing between mermaids and sirens. Write about the first battle.
3. A prince needs a magical lantern in order to complete a task.
4. Write about different kinds of centaur, not just a horse - tiger, deer, etc.
5. The nightingale is a story about an emperor who prefers his mechanical nightingale over the real one. Write from the perspective of the real bird, who is immensely jealous.
6. Medusa - who these days hides her "hair" underneath hats - is a world famous sculptress. She's just been invited to a popular TV show for an interview on her artistic process.
7. A dragon, who hears voices, gives the king an urgent message.
8. For years, you've known about the nymphs living by the lake near your house. You've only just realized they aren't as friendly as they seem.
9. A wizard finds himself far from home, lost and alone.
10. The witch from Hansel and Gretel has a twin sister - and she's furious at the hate witches get because of her evil sister.
11. Beauty is sent to kill the Beast. She's been training for this moment for years.

12. You receive a bottle of pixie dust on your front doorstep. You also find you're allergic to it.
13. A reverse on Swan Lake - a normal swan is cursed to spend her days as a human.
14. The genie has bad intentions and swore to punish his next master, but Aladdin doesn't know it yet.
15. A witch finds she can't brew her potions anymore.
16. The boy and the wolf are working together, and each attempt the boy cries wolf is a ploy for the wolf to attack the village.
17. Peter Pan is the enemy, and Tinkerbell is trying to warn Wendy before it's too late.
18. Goldilocks goes to court for breaking and entering.
19. Cinderella quickly realizes she was only infatuated with the prince and never really loved him.
20. The goose girl leads a coup against the false princess.
21. After slaying the giant, Jack takes over the world in the sky and becomes king. A rather corrupt one at that.
22. A princess needs forgiveness in order to break a magical spell.
23. After being saved from the Big Bad Wolf, Little Red Riding Hood trains under the huntsman.
24. You're a changeling and are trying your best to keep this from your significant other.
25. Masque of the Red Death a prince hosts party to escape a dangerous plague known as the Red Death. Write from the perspective of the Red Death, who joins in on the festivities.
26. A vampire must awaken a curse in order to save her family.

27. Hades and Persephone are going through a tough time. Write from the perspective of their marriage counsellor.
28. A princess is sent to rescue a prince from a dragon, not knowing the two are working together.
29. Aphrodite gets her first grey hair.
30. You fall into a hole and tumble into a dark cavern. The first person you see is an adult woman named Alice. "You shouldn't be here," she says with fear in her eyes.
31. You're the Curse Writer, charging witches and wizards hefty prices for some of your most creative curses.
32. Deep in the darkened tunnels an egg is found. It is a new type of dragons egg.
33. The enchanted forest starts fading away. Why? And whom does this affect the most?
34. Twin waterfalls reveal a hidden kingdom. What sort of people live on the other side?
35. A fire destroys an area of woodlands, leaving at its centre, one lone house, completely untouched.
36. The ice princess has had her heart stolen. What would she be willing to do to get it back?
37. The ice queen drinks from a goblet of ice and is burnt to a crisp.
38. A still lake hides many secrets. What or who walks from the lake today?
39. A school boy steals his headmasters cloak because it's raining, only to find when he puts it on, it gives him the power to hear peoples' thoughts.
40. The fireflies fly and converge on a magical tree when a royal is about to be born. Tonight they

converge on the tree, but the Queen is not giving birth.

41. A crystal cavern holds many secrets. A band of thieves break in and steal three crystals. Death and destruction follow them as they take the three crystals out into the world.

42. The potion was made from three leathers of the last unicorn.

43. A maiden finds a gemstone in the forest and turns it into a charm on a necklace. It's a magical but evil stone.

44. The princess had fallen ill. A curse was said to have befallen her. What unusual curse can you think of and how could she be saved?

45. Magic is gone forever now. We must live on without it.

46. Three sisters, triplets prophesies the king's death. When it comes to pass, each sister now prophesies a different future for the kingdom.

47. A morning star shines bright one morning only to burn all day, growing bigger and bigger, until a second sun burns in the sky.

48. A king listens to a small rat, telling him of the evil to come. The king believes the rat over everyone else.

49. The golden eggs were not what people thought. Golden dragons would be born if only they hadn't been stolen from their mother.

50. At last we've come home. But it is not the home we remember.

50 Myth & Legend/Fairy Tale Story Starters

1. He sighed. "They went to the Underworld again."
2. "I've heard so much about you!" "Good things I hope!" "Well... there was that thing about your centaur parents."
3. Let's just be honest, there's nothing special about Hercules. And no, I'm not jealous of him.
4. "The princess must hang. There's no other way."
5. "I came here to avoid Loki, not have dinner with him."
6. That morning, Rapunzel grabbed scissors she found hidden in a drawer and walked to the mirror.
7. The Loch Ness monster lost her family years ago. Luckily, she has us.
8. "I think you'll find things have changed much since you left. For one, no one is happy to see you. Especially Poseidon."
9. This would be Shahrazad's final story. She had run out of things to say.
10. The Little Mermaid found a quill, ink, and parchment. She spent all night writing.
11. "Behold - the last witch of Camelot."
12. For the first time in his life, Merlin had no idea what to do.
13. "Steal from the rich, give to the poor?" Little John laughed. "That's the farthest from the truth."
14. "If you wish upon a star, at most, you're going to get disappointment."
15. The Brothers Grimm and Hans Christian Andersen become good friends.
16. Apparently, nothing was learned from Midas.

17. Thunder rolled in the sky as lightning struck. It would seem the Gods were angry.
18. I only wanted to get out of the rain. So, I faked everything; even feeling the pea underneath my mattress.
19. "In all, it was a mistake." "I'm glad you realize that." "A good mistake, though."
20. Snow White decided to take her revenge against the evil queen. It was time.
21. A Minotaur ravaging through the city was honestly the least of our concerns.
22. The twelve dancing princesses forced their subjects to dance with them.
23. "I can't challenge the Gods, do you know what they'd do to me?"
24. The nutcracker began to cry, slow and soft tears that no one would hear.
25. "He's a good person." "He's tried to kill us, multiple times." "We all have our faults."
26. Pandora tried to shatter the box, but that only made things worse.
27. "The seventh prince will unite us all."
28. The bogeyman was lonely. He left his home, slinking in search of companionship.
29. My prince, I'm pregnant.
30. The fairy stood her ground. She would end it this day.
31. The magic dried up on the 15th of every month.
32. The fourth day was the worse, converting to witchhood was never said to be easy.
33. The night never came.

34. The dancing elves danced every full moon. But this moon was different, and everyone stayed inside.
35. The king fakes his death to escape his crazy family, leaving the kingdom to a villainous and evil family.
36. Guinevere finally accepts that she loves women, not men, and definitely not Arthur.
37. An angel on earth must hide who he really is when he falls in love with a human.
38. An unforgiving princess is rebuffed but for a gorgeous, neighbouring, eligible prince.
39. A king and queen lose their only child to a horrible disease inflicting their kingdom.
40. A dark knight must find a way to escape his pledge and knightly duties.
41. A medieval doctor finds an herbal cure for a simple, but deadly virus. But the witches and sorcerers of the time believe he's a heretic and sentence him to death. In this world, magic - there is no science - only magic and sorcery are the rightly ways of life.
42. An orphan boy is taken in by a kindly gentleman who's actually a villainous sorcerer with unusual plans for the boy.
43. A witch finds out her sister didn't really die after all.
44. A mermaid could lose her magical amulet, which was keeping her a mermaid.
45. A mermaid's best friend, a special sea turtle is captured by pirates.
46. A prince is blinded during a duel for his princess. But she leaves him after his injury.

47. A dwarf loses his magical hammer deep in a shaft in his mine. It's lost forever. What does this mean?
48. An unusual rainbow appears, with the ability to take travellers to another land.
49. An enchanted frog utters a prophecy that the next princess will be killed by her father.
50. A king and queen are stranded on a deserted island.

Notes

_____

_____

_____

_____

_____

_____

_____

_____

_____

_____

_____

_____

_____

_____

CHAPTER FOUR

100 Epic Fantasy Prompts

On the following pages are all sort of epic fantasy story ideas and prompts, designed with the high fantasy, epic style fantasy story in mind. Here you'll find story ideas full of magic and wonder, magicians, warriors, Queens, Emperors, and story ideas of Epic proportions. Common sub-genres which fall under this section include epic fantasy (obviously), high fantasy, adventure fantasy, and Sword and Sorcery.

50 Epic Fantasy Prompts

1. A murdered king returns as a ghost, determined to find his killer.
2. Magic can only be used by one person in the world. To decide who it will be, the games begin.
3. You're the master of shadows. They've bended to your will for years, but now you sense they're growing irritated with your control.
4. Write about a world where cities are in the sky. The catch? Your character lives alone on the ground.
5. Your character has been locked in the empire's prison for years. However, this is for their protection.
6. Four kingdoms are on the brink of war. However, your character, a lowly servant, knows a secret that can put an end to it and save thousands of lives. The catch? They have a very good reason not to say anything.
7. Write about a ragtag group of thieves who are going to steal the King's crown. However, they all suspect one of them could be a spy.
8. Alternately, write about a group of thieves that band together to return something they stole as keeping this item is more dangerous.
9. The chosen one was supposed to save the world. Unfortunately, he actually agrees with the villain and now wants to join him.
10. You're an assassin who's just been hired to kill the King. Your boss is his wife.
11. You're an oracle, and for years everyone has been extolling your powers. The truth? Years ago, the

real oracle disappeared years ago and you're just filling in.

12. Write about an empire where anyone is eligible to rule, as long as they are willing to sacrifice a family member.

13. The sky is falling, but everyone is used to it by now.

14. Members of a raid think they have the upper hand on a small village. However, this village doesn't intend to submit.

15. Song is akin to magic, with users singing to use their magic. Write about a character with the worst singing voice that results in magic that never goes the way they intend.

16. A royal cartographer who, when they draw on a map, they create new places.

17. A family of illusionists who are set on deceiving their entire world.

18. You're determined to find your mother, who disappeared when you were younger. The only challenge is finding which dimension she went to.

19. You're the daughter of an ice giant, but you have yet to inherit any of your father's abilities.

20. The dance of souls has begun. Write about who attends.

21. Write about a court where night drags on for several days.

22. You're a bounty hunter. But instead of killing your targets, you try your best to help them.

23. Write about a prison made of glass. Everyone, even the guards, are terrified of it.

24. You're a banished knight that can weld electricity. You intend to use that to your advantage.

25. Write about an orb that gives the user the ability to see the lifespan of anyone. One day, you accidentally look at your own even though you swore you'd never. You see 6 days and 5 hours.
26. An epic war between two rival families fighting over land and love.
27. Lovers fall in love and run away, only to be chased by their families. They go on an adventure looking for a way to live without their families.
28. The magic was never going to stop. If they didn't do something soon, it would overwhelm them and their entire world.
29. To become king, the boy had to undergo a series of tests. The trials must occur in a mysterious location, but are required in order for him to become the next ruler.
30. Two warring houses are completely destroyed by magic. Which family and which person takes the lead in the new era?
31. A king and a queen have a baby, but the infant is stolen at birth. Magicians have stolen the baby. What do they teach him or her?
32. A boy meets a dwarf and form an unlikely friendship. They go on adventures together, searching for the truth in their world.
33. A magpie arrives at court one day, signalling the start of a new era.
34. Which child accepts the code and follows the path of those before him?
35. Magic is lost as a queen betrays the king. Her knights come to her rescue. What becomes of these knights and the queen?

36. "Time is growing slow. Something is happening in the kingdom. I need people to know what's going on."
37. The magic was running out. It was up to one person to save it.
38. A lost book of magic was found once more, bringing its reader unrivalled magic.
39. The moon disappears one night. How does the fantasy world evolve/change?
40. A thief and a magician join together to find a missing friend.
41. A clock is the instrument of a future curse.
42. Stranded in a desert, a lone ranger searches for a way home.
43. A small boy stuck in an orphanage will do anything to become a magician.
44. A dwarf lost in an enchanted forest must locate a magic flute in order to rescue his family.
45. A reckless clockmaker stuck in a medieval fortress discovers a trouble causing ghost.
46. An overseer stuck in dreamland must escape.
47. A dutiful son must disobey his parent and duty as a knight in order to find his true love.
48. A forgotten god in an alternate earth must find a way to get home.
49. Your hero is stuck on the moon. He was abandoned there by pirates.
50. A war is about to break out. It's up to three to save the world from its impending destruction.

50 Epic Fantasy Story Starters

1. "There's a good reason no one goes to the sorcerer's house, I thought you would have known that by now."
2. I've seen dragons before. But… never quite like this one.
3. Many people knew her, he made sure that they did. He also made sure that they feared her.
4. It's easy. Just go by the wind and you'll get there, eventually.
5. Dance with me. Pretend your world no longer exists.
6. "Tell me your name. I promise I won't tell anyone."
7. Like my mother before me, and her mother, I don't intend to fail.
8. We were alone, but not for long. Soon they would arrive, and everything would change.
9. There are some things she knew she shouldn't share. But she was never good at keeping a secret.
10. The sky thundered, then cracked open.
11. Everyone turned to look at him. A king with no power.
12. The sword glinted in the sunlight. It would serve her well.
13. If you were looking to die, you went to the deserts. A place where no one returned.
14. Once the curtains opened, there was no turning back.
15. He never mentioned the stories. And he would try his best not to.
16. It rained the day the magic returned.

---

17. With the sun above me and fire in my hand, I walked through the doors.
18. The carriage doors swung open and the first thing that came out was a dainty hand covered in blood.
19. One by one, the stars began to fall from the sky.
20. The world was strange and restless, filled with abnormal creatures.
21. The smile on the goblin's face was wide and twisted, stretching farther than she thought smiles should.
22. "This is the last time we're going to an orc for guidance."
23. For some reason, absolutely no one wanted to inherit the throne.
24. "It's your last day here, spend all the gold you want."
25. I shouldn't be alive. And she should have killed me. Neither of those things came true.
26. "It's you - it's always been you. Only you can save us."
27. The last dragon eggs started to hatch today.
28. The Dark Lord finally located his tool of power. There was no stopping him now.
29. These glasses will help you, but only you will know how to use them.
30. "I am not the chosen one, I can't be, I'm just a beggar."
31. I ran outside and threw my hands to the sky. I had never been so angry. The clouds moved and formed above me, moving to the motion of my hands.
32. A robber had just escaped a local village jail, but stops to help a damsel in distress, becoming a very

reluctant hero, and the only solution to her greater problem.

33. We have to travel to the darkest dungeons, forests and swamps. The map showed us where to go. This was going to be one hell of a quest.

34. The warrior guard shoved the twin princesses into the tower and locked them in.

35. A dwarf village was blasted from existence. Survivors are looking for help and homes. Answers are demanded.

36. The stars began to fall one night. Starting to damage the earth and mess up the heavens.

37. Demons appear on medieval earth. Someone, something has let them out, and has given them a mission.

38. The world is ruled by the Rite Empire, an evil superpower. You are part of the resistance.

39. A pair of lost shoes means the end of virtual story time. Who stole the shoes and why?

40. The village was a perfect medieval location. But technology hid just beneath the surface in the disguise of magic.

41. A group of wizards, a core group of the community, are being murdered, one by one.

42. The king had one son. But he was blind, and they turned him out into the wild, unknowing that he was the true saviour of the kingdom.

43. The 7 councils of the 7 worlds are convening today for a secret meeting. The decision made will change everything.

44. An orphan boy is rescued from his group home, taken in by the royal household as a kitchen boy. But he is more than he appears.

45. His family are kidnapped, and he will do anything to save them. ANYTHING.
46. The Elf Queen has her last baby. But the baby is a prophet and sees the future of their people. They are to be wiped out - by the humans.
47. What if the chosen one is actually the chosen one to bring about the end of the worlds? The prophet got it the wrong way around.
48. A magpie is an omen of death. One appears on your doorstep on the morning of your 18th birthday.
49. We have to jump now, or never see anyone again!
50. A village is cursed, and all inhabitants are turned into animals.

Notes

_____

_____

_____

_____

_____

_____

_____

_____

_____

_____

CHAPTER FIVE

100 Modern Fantasy Prompts

This section includes more modern style fantasy prompts, including the newer Urban Fantasy and Paranormal Fantasy sub-genres. Here, I included prompts which involved more modern and contemporary fantasy ideas and themes, such as vampires and werewolves in modern day, modern day witches and magic, and other typical tropes of Urban Fantasy and Paranormal Fantasy.

50 Modern Fantasy (Paranormal, Urban Fantasy) Prompts

1. There exists a vial that will alter the state of reality once a drop falls to the ground. After you lose your job, you decide to get back at your boss.
2. Write about a character who's immortal and decides to pass their boredom by taking extreme and deadly sports.
3. In a world where flowers dictate your future, you're the town's botanist.
4. Write about a character with the ability to enter paintings or photographs. What happens when they enter a painting and try to leave, but can't?
5. Write about a character who's travelled through dimensions so many times, they no longer remember where they are originally from.
6. The Grim Reaper suddenly quits. Your character is looking for a summer job and submits an application.
7. Your character has the ability to see into the future - but only five minutes of it.
8. You awaken in the middle of the night by a text message from an unknown number. It reads: we need you. You're the only one left.
9. Unlike most animal sidekicks in movies and TV shows, your character's cat has no interest in helping them. In fact, this feline is doing everything it can to stop your protagonist.
10. You and your spouse have just moved into your dream home but quickly discover it's the hideout of a band of faeries. You're shocked, but your spouse is surprisingly calm.

11. You're cleaning out your closest when you stumble upon a note with your name on it. It's from your past and future self.

12. Certain tattoos determine your magical power. For your 18th birthday, your parents take you to get your first tattoo.

13. You gain the ability to read minds. Frighteningly, you decide to read everyone's thoughts at once, but everyone is only thinking of your name.

14. The package you ordered online turns out to be a dragon's egg with a large crack in it.

15. Your parents have always forbidden you from going into the basement. When curiosity gets the better of you, you go down there when they're not home. There you find a ghost that looks exactly like you.

16. Write about a character who learns they are a shapeshifter. The catch? They can only change into objects.

17. Your character is a wizard. Write about their first day at a school for humans.

18. Wishes can be granted - but only at the expense of someone you know personally that has what you want.

19. You faint after being out all day in the sun. When you wake up, you have wings.

20. You start a new job and your co-workers seem friendly enough, but you're convinced your boss is a spectre.

21. You're cursed with the ability to only speak lies. Write about what happens on your wedding day.

22. An elf winds up on your doorstep late at night. They plead with you, "Please don't let them find me."

23. The neighbourhood coffee shop is owned by a werewolf. The laundromat is run by a shapeshifting wyvern. Needless to say, this is no ordinary town.

24. You discover you can fly. On a whim, you decide to use your newfound abilities to fight the crime in your violent neighbourhood.

25. You're a firefighter called to put out the flames of a house fire. However, when you arrive, you find a child sits on the ground, sobbing. "I couldn't control it," they weep.

26. Fairies are real. You are in your backyard one day when a fairy starts talking to you, explaining she needs only your help.

27. A vampire appears in your room one night. He is searching for something.

28. Werewolves are real, and there is one in your class, you just know it. For some reason you are drawn to him, which leads you down an unexpected path.

29. Write about a school that only happens at night, for those of nocturnal tendencies - vampires, werewolves, etc.

30. Three students are trapped at magic school who really shouldn't be there.

31. The world is full of night terrors - it's open season on this year's human tragedy, the newly forming vampires. Time to take them out.

32. The gods and goddesses still protect the sacred temples around the world. But someone breaks in and steals the one true mystical object.

---

33. A boy can communicate with animals in the amazon jungle. What happens?
34. A young witch is sent to boarding school while her errant twin sister is sent somewhere else; to delinquent boarding school.
35. Write about a juvenile detention for young witches and wizards. What problems could young delinquent magical beings get into, to end up here?
36. On a school trip abroad, a girl gets tangled up in the magical underworld of sorcery and magic beneath the foreign city.
37. It's the year 2050. Magic is hidden, but becoming more and more open. However, witches, wizards, and immortals are being persecuted.
38. A young boy discovers his powers for wizardry. He then meets his real Uncle; the Headmaster of the elitist Wizardry School in the country.
39. Three young women realise they have something in common when they start having visions of one another. When they meet for the first time at the local witches school, they know they were destined to be together.
40. I know I am special. I have super strength, but I have to hide it. Only my dad knows, and he's found me this special school where I don't have to hide anymore.
41. The King knew something had to give. And it wouldn't be him.
42. I just found out my sister is a witch. Before today, I never knew witches even existed.
43. Magic was free flowing now; everyone could access it.

44. What if you find out your parents aren't really your parents? And you realise you were stolen.
45. What if your father goes missing, and nobody does anything about it, not even your mother?
46. In the land of the heroes, a young boy finds an old merchant with tales of a strange land. That land is Earth. And it is in desperate need of a hero right now.
47. The demons and imps live just below us. What if they've infiltrated Earth somehow and now live among us?
48. The witches have all been destroyed. It's us next.
49. The occult had a special hold over cult members. The leader could make them do almost anything in the name of the devil.
50. A ghost hunter shows up at his home town, looking for answers from his childhood.

50 Modern Fantasy (Paranormal, Urban Fantasy) Story Starters

1. When the sun rises, so will we. We'll try again and again. We won't let them stop us.
2. The silver light washed over his face, making him look ghastly as he sneered.
3. "You're different from everyone else," she said, then glared. "But that makes you far from special."
4. Scream into the void, and hear it scream back.
5. They were bitter, wild, and hunting for blood.
6. "A *blueberry* isn't going to stop a wraith from attacking us!"
7. They have seven days to find their friends. I'll make sure they don't.
8. The first thing you should know: it was the vampire's fault, not mine.
9. They surrounded my house. There was nowhere to run.
10. "This is where I leave you," she smiled sadly. "It's been nice."
11. I found a dragon scale in my backpack that wasn't there before.
12. As it turns out, zombies are actually quite nice. They're good listeners.
13. "If this is the last time I see you, just know I've always hated you."
14. The sign said was a warning. B*eware,* it read, *the phoenix resides here.*
15. To say I was surprised to shapeshift is an understatement.
16. Everything in him told him not to touch the gem, but he didn't listen.

17. "I'm not trying to be possessed right now," I snapped. "I have three papers due and an exam tomorrow that I haven't studied for. *Go away.*"
18. By dawn, the only indication there'd been a fight was the scent of garlic in the air.
19. "I am going to fight them," he shouted. "Even if you won't. It wouldn't be the first time."
20. "If three leprechauns comes to the door, do *not* let them in. Also, I am not here."
21. Dreams were the only escape, the only sanctuary. Until they weren't.
22. "I am not getting on that thing." "You have no other way of getting home, so just stop whining and hop on."
23. The sphinx looked up at the sky and dreamed.
24. I drove the stake through my best friend's heart, tears falling freely down my face.
25. She was devastating. And that's honestly, that's what I hated — and loved — most about her.
26. "I'll do anything to win." A troubled teen witch is willing to do just about anything to gain power.
27. A quiet witchy neighbourhood suddenly finds a human murdered in the town fountain.
28. A boy finds a secret in his basement and must act to protect and save his family.
29. A family of magicians must save their hometown.
30. A lonely vampire falls in love with the worst choice in the world.
31. A baby, a witch, lost...
32. A baby is born with horns, but it's not what anyone thinks.
33. Girl discovers she can do magic at boarding school, away from all her family.

34. A boy transforms for the first time while at school, in the bathroom.
35. A boy discovers he can heal others and bring people back from the dead, but there's a price.
36. A girl discovers her parents are really sorcerers in the modern world.
37. A wizard's wand is stolen.
38. A magician discovers the real reason for his powers.
39. A witch discovers her true parents.
40. A mermaid falls in love with a human.
41. A princess is blackmailed by her evil royal sorcerer.
42. A school girl makes friends with the local urban legend 'beast' in the woods.
43. An athlete breaks his leg. But in the locker room alone, he somehow heals it before his eyes with his hands.
44. The famous anklet had a special power.
45. Time had stopped again. I didn't know how I kept doing it.
46. No one knew the dance had a spell attached to it. This would change everything.
47. The spell book was lost.
48. "You are the love of my life. But you MUST die."
49. Everything changed after I followed my Aunt into her study.
50. I always knew the garden was special, but I never knew quite how much.

Notes

CHAPTER SIX

100 General Fantasy Prompts - all other subgenres

In the following section you will find all the remaining fantasy type prompts that I couldn't fit into the previous main sub-genres of Epic, Myth & Legend/Fairy Tale and Modern Fantasy. In this section, you'll find prompts on dragons, alternate and historical fantasy, and superhero fantasy, plus many, many more.

50 General Fantasy Prompts

1. A spoiled space captain is betrayed by her crew. The only way back home? Traveling on the ship of a rival captain.
2. The Prince of Death is a giant tarantula. He's just chosen you as his newest apprentice (or victim... he'll decide later).
3. Nightmare and Daydream take human forms. However, neither sibling is interested in running the family business of creating dreams.
4. A dragon is the last of its kind and decides to take revenge against dragon slayers.
5. With the power to manipulate water, you become a corrupt pirate with the ability to defeat your enemies.
6. A group of immortals have spent hundreds of years together. One day and without warning, one of them drops dead.
7. Write about a school for necromancers. What happens when you accidentally raise a dead relative, and get enrolled the next day?
8. The sky changes colour based on its mood, and this often correlates to the weather for the day. Everyone is used to seeing blue, yellow, or the occasional red, but one day the sky turns purple.
9. After the villain destroys the world, he stumbles upon a child, cold and alone. He takes them in.
10. War heroes are called back years later to fight again. But this time the enemy is someone they once fought alongside.
11. Write about a girl named Cayenne and her father who sells spices.

12. Write about three princesses. One from land, air, and sea.
13. A sea captain and captain of the guard despise each other. However, they've both been commissioned by the empress to work together.
14. A magical necklace that causes its wearer to weld dark magic accidentally attaches itself to you.
15. Write about a character that struggles to separate fantasy from reality.
16. The villain has been defeated, and the hero is rewarded. However, the hero's friends become concerned when their friend begins to show the same attitudes of their defeated foe.
17. You have the ability to stop time. Usually you use it to make it to work on time or sleep in longer. But this time you've frozen time for so long, that when you try to resume it, time remains frozen.
18. The characters from a book you're reading come to life. For some reason, they all hate you.
19. You discover a hidden passageway in your house that leads to a world that's an exact replica of the one you currently live in. Only you don't exist.
20. There is a forest at the edge of the kingdom that's forbidden to enter. Anyone who went in returned with six deadly jewels. You're poor and desperate for money. You decide to journey to the forest.
21. The hero gets tired of the journey halfway through and quits. Now it's up to you, the weary mentor, to save the world before it's too late.
22. You're a time traveler, and you're pretty knowledgeable about historical events. One day you travel to a time period that's unheard of and has never been mentioned in history books or by

historians. Not to mention the people there aren't surprised to see you.

23. You're a magician with the ability to change people's minds. Why would this be dangerous?

24. A magical codex holds the answer to all of life's questions. Whenever a question is asked, the answer writes itself in the book. You decide to ask a question and the answer is never written.

25. A routine trip to the crypts reveals a man who definitely wasn't there yesterday. And he's relieved to see you.

26. Your character finds a magical tree with the power to grant life and take life.

27. A famous midwife who only births royal heirs is hard at work. But this baby is not a royal heir...

28. A canal is the secret to the palace and this story.

29. A magical knight must leave his home and find the rightful heir to the throne.

30. A dwarf and elf must become friends and fight a common enemy.

31. A boy discovers he has superpowers and tries to find others like him.

32. Magic in the dark, a cavern full of forgotten mysteries and creatures.

33. Write about a kingdom that only appears every 10 years.

34. Write about an ice pond with an unusual monster inside.

35. There is an ice cavern in a high mountain with a strange mystery.

36. What happens at the secret desert oasis, filled with mystical and mythological creatures?

37. An old book is found with the lessons of the past. When readers read it, they are pulled into the world.
38. There was once a library full of magical books.
39. There exists a wishing fountain that reveals your worst fears and makes them come true.
40. The Dark Prince must solve the riddle of his ancestors, before the Light Prince destroys him.
41. A storm brings acid rain, heralding the return of the dragons.
42. A new king arises. The time of the dragons. The people must bend the knee or die.
43. Two men, thieves find a way to reach the king and steal his prize possession -his only daughter/his magic elixir/his magical crown - your choice.
44. A frog finds its way into the castle kitchen. The soup is tainted, and everyone falls deathly ill. What's really going on here?
45. A young princess and her brother are orphaned after a deadly virus. The two young warriors must lead their country and kingdom to safety.
46. An evil queen wants to find true love. What must she do to achieve it?
47. The enchanted forest burns down. What happens to all the magical creatures?
48. A girl from modern day is transported into a storybook and finds herself in a fairy tale.
49. A lost tomb holds the answer to the mystery of a murdered king.
50. The knights find a mysterious tower cover in vines. When they cut them down, it's not what they expect.

50 General Fantasy Story Starters

1. "After everything I've given you, *this* is how you repay me?"
2. Beneath us, the ground shook. It was a sign they had come.
3. In this city, he intended to be the king, working with the shadows.
4. Generally, the rule is to never trust a warlock. There are exceptions, however.
5. "I feel in the mood for some music." "The world is ending." "... So, no soft jazz?"
6. Every day, my guardian angel became more and more disappointed in me. I almost felt bad. Almost.
7. There are three steps you take when you decide to storm a castle. The first step? Reconsider. I wish I'd followed my own advice.
8. "If things don't turn out right, make up something cool I might have said. I want a meaningful headstone."
9. The door was ajar, and that was never a good thing.
10. The siren fell in love, which meant she was definitely in trouble.
11. "Don't get me wrong, I'm happy to see you, but... I thought we agreed no more spell books."
12. "Grow, my darling. You have nothing else better to do."
13. The wand snapped in half, the sound of it silencing the entire room.
14. The paper fluttered into her hands; the edges rimmed in gold.

15. "Are butterflies normally this size?" "No... but then, what here is normal?"
16. Several foxes surrounded the man, snarling, while he looked at them with mild amusement.
17. "I believe this is where we part. I would say it's been a pleasure, but..."
18. All elixirs weren't dangerous, but this one clearly was.
19. Lights flashed above them, a warning that something was coming.
20. Here, in the shadow of my thoughts, I learned to be brave.
21. The duke fell to the ground amid shocked gasps from the crowd.
22. Golden sunlight fell on the battlefield and somewhere, a child began to wail.
23. "Magic is not to be played with," The masked girls said in unison. "It is to be conquered with."
24. She may be mortal, but she had more cunning than all of them.
25. Time can be manipulated, if you know how.
26. A magical castle is atop a lone mountain, reachable only by climbing vines. Who lives in this castle?
27. A boy finds an amulet which gives him magical powers. He must learn to use them and help his people.
28. A book of spells is lost through time. A girl in the middle ages finds it on a fairy mound in a dark forest.
29. A lost princess walks alone through an empty castle.

30. An imp stagers though a magical forest. He finds three people, one who could hurt him, one who could help him, and one he had no idea about.
31. A little mushroom is the home of two elves. Their home is about to be destroyed.
32. A magical forest holds the key to the all the answers of the universe.
33. The creatures of the swamp are angry and will do anything to seek revenge.
34. The lines of dunes stretched forever. He was lost. Done for. And he had only one wish left.
35. The hole in the ground held a mystery that only the goblins knew.
36. The knights of the round table had an odd quest to undertake, and no one could know about it - especially King Arthur.
37. The Queen of the Ice Forest was dying. It would change everything.
38. Last night I got lost walking home. I blacked out. This morning, I am different. There is something growing out of my back.
39. The magician held the orb up to the moon. But nothing happened.
40. The mushrooms were in the secret garden, guarded by flower sprites. Somehow I had to get in there and get those mushrooms.
41. "The King must die. Tonight."
42. A teen cowboy fights for survival on an alternate planet.
43. The ice would protect us, it's never failed us before.
44. The only way out of this is to burn it all.
45. There was a time I loved you. Now you are the most frightening person in the world to me.

46. A blind vampire must help save the world.
47. I found the eggs in a cave. They were glowing, and I took them. I don't regret it.
48. The Gods never disappointed.
49. The Gods never disappeared from humanity. They stayed in human form amongst the humans, biding their time.
50. The dragons have decided on an heir for the kingdom; a human child.

Notes

_____

_____

_____

_____

_____

_____

_____

_____

_____

_____

_____

_____

_____

CHAPTER SEVEN

100 Fantasy Title Prompts

Following are 100 Fantasy Title Prompts that you can use to build a story from. Use these titles to germinate the seed of an idea in your mind, or in a timed writing session.

Remember to develop your idea by creating a character or two, a setting, a conflict, and a desire for your character/s. Once you have these elements, your story will begin to grow.

The title prompts are short phrases, names, or statements designed to be a jumping off point for your writing sessions. Develop an idea using the directions above, or just dive right in and freewrite and see what happens.

Good luck and happy writing!

1. The Magic House
2. The Undea Magnet
3. Watchdog
4. Unforgiven
5. Untainted
6. Unexpected Love
7. Love Returned
8. Love Gone
9. The Emperors Rein
10. Nighttime Terrors
11. The Ruins Of Azabr
12. The Cit of Gods
13. The Ruler
14. Magician Zero
15. Rocks Galore
16. Below Wild
17. Into the Zone
18. Twilight Fever
19. Unconceivable Quest
20. The Hunt for Maggie Smith
21. The Hunt Huntress
22. Corrupt Witches
23. Magnificent Crimes
24. Along for the Ride
25. The Innocents
26. Crabapple Tree Time
27. The Memories
28. The Swamp
29. Fever
30. Ratchett
31. Becoming
32. Unbecoming
33. Being Death

34. Death Calls
35. The Dragon's Tooth
36. The Hunters Tribe
37. The Huntress' Sister
38. The Queen's Lover
39. The King's Mistress
40. The Mine Slavers
41. The Case of...
42. A Tale of Mirrors
43. A Tale of Horrors
44. Mirror Magic
45. Night Magic
46. The Scent of the Sea
47. A World Beneath
48. The Unending Story
49. Wolf Magic
50. A Tale of Time and Night
51. Samy and the Magic Key
52. A Story of Time
53. Ancients Lost
54. Ancients Remembered
55. The Three Sisters
56. A Time of Lost Cities
57. The Lost City
58. The Faerie Princess
59. The Lost Map of Paradise
60. The Dragon Priestess
61. The God of Light
62. A Dragon's Curse
63. The Time Games
64. The Trials of Magic
65. The Dragon Chronicles
66. The Dragon Lock

100. Boy of the Runes

Notes

_____

_____

_____

_____

_____

_____

_____

_____

_____

_____

_____

_____

_____

_____

_____

_____

_____

_____

CHAPTER EIGHT

Summary

I hope you enjoyed these fantasy writing prompts. Don't forget, just use what you want, and you never have to use the whole prompt. Even blend the prompts if you like.

If you'd like more prompts, check out thebusywritersnotebook.com, where I have new writing prompts each month.

Sign up for my mailing list to be notified when new prompts are posted, and when I have a new writing prompt book out. Sign up at https://bit.ly/2JbLa6o, and you'll receive a bonus 30 Epic Fantasy Prompts!

If you enjoyed this book, I'd really appreciate it if you could leave me a short review on Amazon. I'd love to hear your thoughts and feedback.

Happy Writing!

Erica

About The Author

Erica Blumenthal is a long-time lover of science fiction, fantasy, old school dystopian fiction and apocalyptic fiction, and more recently urban fantasy. Erica writes under the pen name Candence Stone, and is currently working on her first YA Fantasy series. She blogs about writing, writing resources, and writing prompts at thebusywritersnotebook.com. She has a Masters of Science in Geology, and currently lives in the South West of WA in Australia with her daughter and partner.

Printed in Great Britain
by Amazon

67061543R00041